Artists in Their Time

Edward Hopper

Emma Foa

Franklin Watts
A Division of Scholastic Inc.
New York Toronto London Auckland Sydney
Mexico City   New Delhi   Hong Kong
Danbury, Connecticut

First published in 2003 by
Franklin Watts
96 Leonard Street
London EC2A 4XD

First American edition published
in 2003 by Franklin Watts
A Division of Scholastic Inc.
90 Sherman Turnpike
Danbury, CT 06816

Series Editor: Adrian Cole
Editor: Susie Brooks
Series Designer: Mo Choy
Art Director: Jonathan Hair
Picture Researcher: Sue Mennell

A CIP catalog record for this title
is available from the Library of Congress.

ISBN 0-531-12240-9 (Lib. Bdg.)
ISBN 0-531-16641-4 (Pbk.)

Printed in Hong Kong, China

Acknowledgements

Art Institute of Chicago/Corbis: 33 (Francis G. Mayer). Arthayer and Ruth Sanborn Collection: 6t, 6b, 8t, 36t. Brooklyn Museum of Art, New York/Bridgeman Art Library: 18t. © 1989 Center for Creative Photography, Arizona Board of Regents (photograph by Louise Dahl-Wolfe): 17t, 32t. Center for Creative Photography, the University of Arizona/photograph by Hans Namuth/© 1991 Hans Namuth Estate: 26t, 38t. © The Cleveland Museum of Art, 2002 (Gift of Miss Amelia Elizabeth White, 164.160) :7. Corbis: fr cover bc and 20t (Underwood and Underwood), fr cover br and 24t, 26b (Robert Holmes), 28t (Hulton/Deutsch Collection), 33 (Francis G. Mayer), 35 (Francis G. Mayer). Des Moines Art Center, Des Moines, Iowa/Corbis: fr cover and 21 (Francis G. Mayer). Digital Images © 2002 Museum of Modern Art, New York/Scala, Florence: 29, 31, 36b © ADAGP, Paris and DACS, London 2003. Courtesy of the Gagosian Gallery, New York: 39. Neil Greentree: 37. Hirshhorn Museum and Sculpture Garden, Smithsonian Institute, Washington D.C., Burstein Collection/Corbis: 15. Hugh Lane Municipal Gallery of Modern Art, Dublin/Bridgeman Art Library: 9. Hulton Archive: fr cover bl and 13b, 22t, 30t, 32b. Milwaukee Art Museum Purchase Acquisition Fund (M1965.34) photographed by Efraim Lev-er:16. Montgomery Museum of Fine Arts, Montgomery, Alabama: 19. Musée de la Ville de Paris, Musée Carnavalet/Bridgeman Art Library: 8b. Musée du Louvre, Paris/Bridgeman Art Library: 38b. © Museum of the City of New York (93.1.1.4990): 10t. Museum of Fine Arts, Houston, Texas, USA/Bridgeman Art Library 14b © The Lane Collection, Museum of Fine Arts, Boston, MA. © 2002 Board of Trustees, National Gallery of Art, Washington: 20b (Collection of Mr and Mrs Paul Mellon), 27 (John Hay Whitney Collection). The Newark Museum (on extended loan from the collection of the Port Authority of New York and New Jersey)/Art Resource, NY: 25t © ARS, NY and DACS, London 2003. Peter Newark's American Pictures: 24b. Pollock-Krasner House and Study Center, New York: 25b © Estate of Hans Namuth. Philadelphia Museum of Art, Pennsylvania/Bridgeman Art Library: 22b. Rheinisches Bildarchiv/Museum Ludwig, Cologne: 40b © ARS, NY and DACS, London 2003. Rijksmuseum Kroller-Muller, Otterlo/Bridgeman Art Library: 10b. Ronald Grant Archive: 28b (Paramount Pictures), 41. Saatchi Collection, London/Bridgeman Art Library: 30b © The Andy Warhol Foundation for the Visual Arts, Inc./ARS, New York and DACS, London 2003. Trademarks licensed by the Campbell Soup Company. All Rights Reserved. Seavest Collection of Contemporary American Realism: 40t ©Robert Cottingham, courtesy of the Forum Gallery, New York. © Estate of Sidney Waintrob: 12. Smithsonian American Art Museum, Washington D.C./Art Resource, NY: 18b. © 2002 The Estate and Foundation of Andy Warhol/DACS, London 2003. Collection of the Whitney Museum of American Art, New York: 11 (Josephine N. Hopper Bequest),14t (Gift of Gertrude Vanderbilt Whitney),17b (Bequest of Josephine N. Hopper),23,34 (Josephine N. Hopper Bequest) ,42 (Bequest of Josephine N. Hopper). Photograph supplied by the Whitney Museum of American Art: 13t (cover designed by Edward Hopper for The Morse Dry Dock Dial, 2 published by Morse Dry Dock and Repair Company, Brooklyn,N.Y.), 36t (private collection). Yale University Art Gallery/Corbis: 35 (Francis G. Mayer).

Whilst every attempt has been made to clear copyright
should there be any inadvertent omission please apply
in the first instance to the publisher regarding rectification.

Contents

Who Was Edward Hopper?   6

Impressions of Paris   8

In the Symbolist Style   10

Etcher and Printmaker   12

Success as a Painter   14

Jo Verstille Nivison   16

Summers by the Sea   18

The Silent Observer   20

Hopper's New York   22

The New Deal   24

Cape Cod   26

The Movies   28

On the Road   30

The Restaurant Theme   32

Ignoring the War   34

Painting Sunlight   36

The Final Curtain   38

Hopper's Legacy   40

Artistic Accounts   42

Timeline   42

Glossary   44

Museums and Galleries   45

Index   46

Who Was Edward Hopper?

Edward Hopper was a quiet, reclusive man who became one of the best known artists of 20th-century America. His style was called "Realism" because he painted ordinary, everyday subjects in a realistic way – but his work was far from ordinary. Hopper's paintings are full of atmosphere and feeling, and give us a very personal picture of the world the artist lived in.

GROWING UP

Hopper was born on July 22, 1882, in Nyack, a small town on the Hudson River in New York state. He grew up in a modest, comfortable house which his grandfather built. His father was a hardworking merchant and his mother was a devout Baptist. He had a sister, Marion, who was two years older than he was.

▲ This is Edward Hopper at eight years old with his sister Marion, age ten.

▲ The Hoppers' house at 53 North Broadway, stood at the top of Nyack's Main Street. Buildings such as this one appear in many of the artist's paintings.

A LONELY GIANT

Hopper spent most of his childhood reading, sailing, and most of all, drawing. He attended local schools, helped out at his father's store, and spent many happy hours at the town's bustling boatyards.

The young Hopper was a loner, and remained one throughout his life. One of the things that singled him out was his height.

By the age of 12 he was a staggering 6 feet (1.8 m) tall and still had 5 inches (12 cm) to grow. This lonely boy was to become the giant of American Realism.

DEVELOPING TALENT

At the age of 17 Hopper entered the Correspondence School of Illustrating, and the following year transferred to the New York School of Art. His parents wanted him to study graphic design but he was more interested in painting.

At the New York School of Art Hopper found himself in impressive company – fellow students included future famous names such as George Bellows (1882-1925), Guy Pène du Bois (1884-1958), and Rockwell Kent (1894-1978) – plus an inspirational teacher, Robert Henri (1865-1929).

"Few teachers of art have got as much out of their pupils, or given them as great an initial impetus."

Edward Hopper talking about his
teacher Robert Henri

THE ASHCAN SCHOOL

Robert Henri was radical in his teaching methods and views. He rejected the idea of "art for art's sake" and urged a more realistic approach to painting, claiming that "art cannot be separated from life." He believed that art had the power and duty to communicate with everyone, not just decorate the homes of the rich. He taught his students to look at aspects of everyday urban life as subjects for their art. Hopper always remembered his teacher's enthusiasm and encouragement.

Henri was the founder of what was called the Ashcan School. Ash cans were old-fashioned containers that were used to store the ashes of coal fires. They were very ordinary, everyday objects. The Ashcan School of painting represented ordinary, everyday subjects such as bleak urban scenes, people at work, and life in the slums.

▲ *A Woman's Work,* 1912, John Sloan (1871-1951). This everyday scene, a view from the artist's window, is typical of the Ashcan School. We can almost hear the clothes flapping in the breeze.

Impressions of Paris

After five years at the New York School of Art, Hopper worked for a few months as an illustrator for an advertising agency. It wasn't a happy time for Hopper, but he began saving money for a trip to Paris, the art capital of the world. He eventually made it to Paris with help from his parents in October of 1906.

SKETCHING THE STREETS

Hopper did not share the Bohemian lifestyle of the other artists in Paris. His parents found him a place to stay in a Baptist mission and he didn't enroll in a French art school. Instead, under the guidance of

▲ Hopper enjoyed sketching (as shown here in 1907) in Paris. The French capital had more effect on him than any other city in Europe.

"I was a rotten illustrator – or mediocre anyway."

Edward Hopper

▶ *The Steps at the Rue Alboni,* c.1897, A. Durbec. Paris at the turn of the century was an elegant city where people would stroll the streets dressed in fashionable clothes. This period became known as the "Belle Epoque."

TIMELINE ▶

July 22, 1882	1899–1900	1900–06	1906	1907
Edward Hopper is born in Nyack, New York.	Hopper attends the Correspondence School of Illustrating in New York.	Hopper studies graphic design and painting at the New York School of Art.	Hopper works as a commercial artist in New York City. In October he travels to Paris and stays at a Baptist Mission at 48 Rue de Lille.	Hopper travels to London, the Netherlands, Berlin, and Brussels. He stops again in Paris before returning to New York.

Patrick Henry Bruce, a fellow student of Henri, Hopper discovered the work of the Impressionists. This inspired him to sketch as he explored the city. He worked on the spot, using charcoal, watercolor, and oils. He painted streets, buildings, bridges, and people. He was also fascinated by Parisian characters such as police officers, soldiers, and people in cafés.

> *"I do not believe there is another city on Earth so beautiful as Paris."*
>
> *Edward Hopper*

IMPRESSIONISM

Impressionism is a style of painting which originated in France in the 1860s and had an enormous impact on Western art. Leaders in this movement included Paul Cézanne (1839-1906), Edgar Degas, Claude Monet, Camille Pissarro (1863-1944), and Pierre-Auguste Renoir (1841-1919). These artists sought to capture a particular moment – an "impression" of what the eye sees rather than a faithful, detailed record of the subject. Hopper especially admired

ART WORLD UNFOLDS

Hopper traveled to London, then on to the Netherlands, Berlin, and Brussels before returning to Paris. The Paris art scene was buzzing with new movement – there was Fauvism with its wild, unnatural colors; Cubism with its fragmented, rearranged forms; and the beginning of Abstraction. Two radical artists were also in Paris – Henri Matisse (1869-1954) and Pablo Picasso (1881-1973) – but Hopper said, "They made no particular impression on me."

He preferred the rich realism of 19th-century painters such as Gustave Courbet (1819-77) and Édouard Manet (1832-83), and the use of shimmering light by Impressionists such as Edgar Degas (1834-1917) and Claude Monet (1840-1926).

▲ *Waterloo Bridge, Cloudy Day*, **1900, Claude Monet.**
Monet painted everyday scenes such as bridges and railroad stations over and over again, at different times of day and in different weather conditions. Hopper shared his interest in changing light and the effect it had on different surfaces.

Edgar Degas, whose use of strangely cropped and off-center compositions eventually found its way into Hopper's own work. Monet was another favorite. A number of Hopper's Paris scenes share a striking similarity with Monet's in their use of sunlight and loose, broken brushwork. Hopper spoke later about the lasting effect his time in Paris had on him. In 1962, at age 80, he admitted, "I think I'm still an Impressionist."

In the Symbolist Style

Symbolism was an art movement which flourished in France toward the end of the 19th century. Symbolist painters rejected the "frothy" realism of Impressionist art — they wanted to portray deeper, more meaningful ideas. They looked to images from mythology and dreams to find "a visual language of the soul," and used symbols to represent these deeper meanings. Their ideas were mirrored in the studies of dreams and the unconscious mind by Sigmund Freud and Carl Jung. Gustave Moreau (1826-98) and Odilon Redon (1840-1916) were two of the leading Symbolist painters.

▲ Hopper's home at 3 Washington Square North, in New York, pictured here c.1900.

▲ *Pegasus Triumphant*, 1905-07, Odilon Redon. Pegasus, the winged horse from Greek mythology, is seen here defeating Hydra, the nine-headed serpent. It is an eerie, dreamlike image typical of the Symbolist style.

Hopper loved his time in Paris but New York was his home. He returned there in 1910, rented a room on East 59th Street, and reluctantly took a job as a commercial artist. He only worked a three-day week so that he could paint the rest of the time. In 1913 he moved into an apartment at 3 Washington Square North, which remained his New York address for the rest of his life.

REJECTED

In 1914, Hopper completed *Soir Bleu* (opposite). When it was exhibited at New York's MacDowell Club in February of 1915, the painting was badly received. It was judged to be a poor imitation of French Symbolist art and Hopper never showed it again. Nevertheless, we catch glimpses of what was to come in its lost and lonely figures and use of a horizontal format.

TIMELINE ▶

1909	1910	1913	August 4, 1914	1915
Hopper visits Paris for a few months and paints outdoors by the River Seine.	Back in New York, Hopper is included in an "Exhibition of Independent Artists." In May he visits Europe again.	In March, Hopper sells his first painting, *Sailing*, for $250. Later he moves to 3 Washington Square North.	War breaks out in Europe, with France, Russia, and Britain on one side and Germany and Austria-Hungary on the other.	Hopper takes up etching. In February he shows *Soir Bleu* at the MacDowell Club of New York.

Soir Bleu, 1914

oil on canvas, 36 x 72 in (91.4 x 182.9 cm), Whitney Museum of American Art,
New York, New York

This café terrace scene is filled with French characters – an elegant couple in evening wear,
a thoughtful, lonely figure smoking, and a madam that is surveying the gathering. Some of
the figures are symbolic. For example, Hopper includes a tired-looking clown dressed in
white, which probably represents him.

The way the figures dominate the picture is unusual for Hopper – but they all appear to
be occupied in their individual thoughts which is typical of Hopper's style.

"It seemed awfully crude and raw here when I got back.
It took me ten years to get over Europe."

Edward Hopper

Etcher and Printmaker

Opportunities for artists were scarce during World War I and the years that followed – there were fewer places to show work and less money to spend on it.

Hopper decided to branch out. In 1915 he took up etching since there was a growing market for it. Etching is a form of printmaking.

◀ Hopper in his New York studio, 1955. Behind him is his etching *Railroad Crossing*, done in 1923. In this etching Hopper uses heavy lines to create the effect of blustery darkness, while a lonely figure and his cow appear spotlit, center stage.

A NEW TECHNIQUE

Hopper was introduced to the etching technique by fellow artist Martin Lewis. The pair were similar in many ways. They were close in age, both supported their love of painting with money from commercial work, and they chose many of the same subjects to paint – such as buildings, trains, and railroad stations. More importantly, Lewis was an etcher. Under his guidance, Hopper bought all the materials he needed and began to experiment. He even found that etching

THE ETCHING PROCESS

Etching is a form of printmaking which involves scratching a picture onto a wax-covered metal plate. The plate is placed into a bath of acid which eats away, or "etches," the metal, but only where the lines have been scratched. Afterward, the plate is cleaned and rolled with ink so that the etched lines fill with ink. The picture can then be easily printed onto paper again and again.

TIMELINE ▶

March 1917	April 1917	June 27, 1917	1918	November 11, 1918
The start of the Russian Revolution.	President Woodrow Wilson declares war on Germany in order to "save democracy." Hopper exhibits at the First Annual Exhibition of the American Society of Independent Artists.	The first U.S. troops land in France to help the Allies.	Hopper's etchings are included in several exhibitions. In October he wins first prize for his poster *Smash the Hun*.	The armistice is signed, signaling the end of World War I.

helped his painting.

Etching suited Hopper's background in illustration as well as his love of contrasts. He liked the way the dark lines of the ink contrasted with the white paper.

Hopper produced dozens of etchings between 1915 and 1923. He won numerous prizes, gaining the recognition as an etcher that he had failed to achieve as a painter so far.

> *"After I took up etching, my paintings seemed to crystallize."*
>
> Edward Hopper

▲ *Smash the Hun,* Hopper's prizewinning war poster of 1918, appeared on the front cover of the *Morse Dial* shipping magazine in February 1919.

SMASH THE HUN, WAR POSTER

From 1914 to 1918, Europe was embroiled in World War I. In April of 1917, the U.S. joined in the fight against Germany. U.S. troops were sent to France to help the Allies.

▲ U.S. troops leaving New York for the battlefields of Europe, 1917.

In 1918 the U.S. Shipping Board ran a wartime poster competition to raise people's awareness about the war. Over 1,400 entries were received. Even though Hopper was not interested in politics, he submitted *Smash the Hun* ("Hun" was a slang word for a German). Although Hopper created this powerful anti-German poster, he defended German poster design saying, "Poster technique in Germany has been carried to a perfection that has been attained in no other country."

Hopper won the $300 first prize in the competition – more than he had ever received for a painting! His success brought him considerable attention from the press. One newspaper identified him as a "well-known illustrator" – not necessarily true at the time but it would have pleased Hopper.

Success as a Painter

Hopper was fascinated by the different times of day, and especially by the presence or absence of sunlight. Many of his paintings, including *Eleven A.M.*, specified an hour in the title. What mattered more than the time was light. Hopper linked the quality of light with moods. Strong sunlight with piercing brightness and dramatic shadows suggested hopefulness to him. On the other hand, morning and evening light with soft tones and cool shadows had an air of mystery or even menace.

▲ Strong diagonal shadows, as shown in this photograph by artist Charles Sheeler (1883-1965), appear again and again in Hopper's work.

Despite the success of his etchings, Hopper struggled for recognition as a painter. His first solo exhibition at the Whitney Studio Club in 1920 did not produce a single sale. In 1924, the 42-year-old artist's fortunes changed.

◀ The Whitney Studio Club opened in New York in 1918, as part of a program to boost contemporary American art. Hopper attended their evening sketching classes, such as the one shown here by Peggy Bacon in 1923.

A PAINTER AT LAST

In November of 1924, Hopper exhibited 11 watercolors at the Frank K. M. Rehn Gallery in New York. He sold every painting, plus an additional five. His art was an overnight sensation. At last Hopper felt secure enough to give up his commercial work and concentrate on painting full-time.

This huge turnaround closely followed another change in Hopper's life – his marriage to Jo Nivison. Jo found her way into his heart and into his art. She posed as the woman in *Eleven A.M.*, and for all Hopper's paintings from then on.

RECURRING THEMES

In *Eleven A.M.* we see some of Hopper's favorite themes – the combination of a lone woman, a window, and sunlight. Windows always interested Hopper. He liked the idea of showing the inside and outside of a building at the same time – something that relatively few artists have attempted.

TIMELINE ▶

January 1920	February 1923	December 1923	July 9, 1924	November 1924
Hopper's first solo show at the Whitney Studio Club, 147 West 4th Street.	Hopper displays work at the Exhibition of Etchers, Art Institute of Chicago. He wins the Logan prize.	Hopper makes his second sale: the Brooklyn Museum purchases his watercolor, *The Mansard Roof*.	Edward Hopper marries Josephine Verstille Nivison at a church on West 16th Street. Fellow artist Guy Pène du Bois is best man.	Hopper sells 16 watercolors and finally gives up commercial work.

Eleven A.M., 1926

oil on canvas, 28 x 36 in (71.3 x 91.6 cm), Hirshhorn Museum and Sculpture Garden, Smithsonian Institution, Washington, D.C.

This picture is full of mystery. We find ourselves asking questions as we look at the woman. Why is she only wearing shoes? What is she thinking about? What is her mood?

Perhaps we feel that the woman looks vulnerable because she is unclothed. We also feel guilty that we are watching her, invading her privacy. The woman seems drawn away from the darkness of the room toward the bright sunlight outside, as she sits leaning forward with her face hidden behind her hair. Perhaps the painting is about the loneliness of big city life, a typical Hopper theme.

"I wanted to achieve the sensation for which so few artists try, of the interior and exterior of a building seen simultaneously."

Edward Hopper

Jo Verstille Nivison

Josephine Verstille Nivison first met Edward Hopper at the New York School of Art. He had returned there to visit his former teacher Robert Henri, who was now Jo's teacher.

Later she found that Hopper shared her love of literature, films, theater, the countryside, and most importantly, painting.

▲ *The Art Student*, 1906, Robert Henri.
Henri painted this portrait of Jo while she was a student at the New York School of Art.

EARLY PROMISE

Josephine was born in New York in 1883. At the age of 17, she enrolled at the Normal College of the City of New York (now Hunter College) – a free institution for women who wanted to become teachers. She had energy, intelligence, and talent. She threw herself wholeheartedly into everything.

She studied Latin, French, English Literature, U.S. History, Psychology, and the Principles of Education. She also performed in a variety of plays and produced numerous drawings for the school magazine and yearbook. After graduating she enrolled at the New York School of Art to study under Robert Henri.

OPPOSITES ATTRACT

In many ways Jo and Edward's relationship was an attraction of opposites. Jo was tiny and birdlike in appearance; Hopper was a towering giant. Jo had a bubbly, chatty, and outgoing personality; Hopper was quiet, serious, and self-contained. She once described "talking with Eddie" as "just like dropping a stone in a well, except that it doesn't thump when it hits the bottom." However, their common interests in theater and the arts bound them together.

A MODEL WIFE

Although Jo was a painter, it was clear from early on that her husband was going to be more successful than she. She supported him and helped promote his work. She shopped for props and kept a faithful record of all his etchings and paintings (see page 44).

Jo's involvement in Hopper's art went far deeper. She was very possessive of Hopper, and in the time they were together refused to let him paint other women. As a result, Jo posed for all of his female figures, from the nude girls looking out of windows to the bored usherettes, to the female clown bowing to the audience in Hopper's final painting. She was truly a model wife.

Jo and Edward Hopper in 1933, nine years after their marriage. Jo was one of the few people Hopper became close to. Although they often argued, she was very loyal to Hopper.

"Ed is the very center of my universe… If I'm on the point of being very happy, he sees to it that I'm not."

Jo Hopper

Edward Hopper at His Easel, c.1930, Jo Nivison. This is one of many pictures that Jo painted of Hopper at work.

ARTISTIC PARTNERSHIP

In 1923, Jo was invited to submit some of her watercolors for an exhibition to be held at the Brooklyn Museum. She accepted but also recommended that they exhibit some of Hopper's work. The Museum ended up taking six of her watercolors and six of Hopper's. It was the beginning of a collaboration that would last for 44 years.

Jo married Hopper in 1924 and moved into his somewhat basic apartment at 3 Washington Square North. She fit perfectly into his lifestyle. She cooked simple meals, usually canned beans or pea soup, bought clothes in discount stores, and accepted her husband's insistence on driving cheap, secondhand cars. They became an inseparable pair.

Summers by the Sea

▲ *The Mansard Roof* was one of six watercolors Hopper showed at the Brooklyn Museum in 1923, alongside paintings by his wife Jo. The Museum purchased it for $100. It was his first sale in ten years!

WATERCOLORS

Hopper started using watercolors in 1923, painting enthusiastically during summers in New England. He had little success with oil paintings, which usually took him months to complete. Having discovered his talent for watercolor painting, as proved by his success at the Rehn Gallery in 1924 (see page 14), Hopper found he could finish a picture in just one sitting.

Hopper's subjects were typical seaside scenes, but without people – bare, white wooden houses and churches, and flamboyant mansions with unusual geometric angles and intricate architectural details. He also painted nautical scenes – boats and water – and, of course, lighthouses.

After 1910, Hopper never visited Europe again. He usually spent the winter months at his home in New York and the summers in New England. Cape Elizabeth, Maine, quickly became one of his favorite summer spots.

TWO LIGHTS

Two Lights is a rocky point on Cape Elizabeth. Hopper made a number of watercolors there, painting the Coast Guard station, the cottages, and the 131-foot (40-m) high lighthouse towering over the landscape. The famous artist Winslow Homer (1836-1910) had lived a few miles away. Homer looked to the sea for inspiration rather than the land. He painted the forces of nature such as surf lashing against the rocks. Hopper was more interested in man-made structures, especially the way strong sunlight played against the walls of buildings. People were rarely featured in these scenes. The buildings are left to speak for themselves.

▲ *High Cliff, Coast of Maine*, 1894, Winslow Homer. Homer concentrated on the wildness of nature, in contrast to the stillness of Hopper's scenes.

TIMELINE ▶

1925	1926	1927	August 1927	January 1928
Hopper exhibits work at the 10th Annual Exhibition of the Whitney Studio Club.	St. Botolph Club, Boston, puts on an "Exhibition of Watercolors and Etchings by Edward Hopper," with 19 watercolors and 21 etchings.	The Hoppers buy a car. They spend the summer at Two Lights in Cape Elizabeth, Maine.	The *Jazz Singer* is released in the U.S. It's the first "talkie" – a film with sound.	Hopper produces his last print, *Portrait of Jo*.

Light at Two Lights, 1927

watercolor on paper, 14 x 40 in (35.5 x 101.6 cm), Collection of Blount, Inc.,
Montgomery, Alabama

The lighthouse dominates this painting, reaching so high into the sky that its top disappears
from view. Its walls are dazzling white and dotted with jet-black windows. Hopper shows
us his love of geometrical forms in the building on the right.

"I like Maine very much, but it gets so cold in the fall...
there's a beautiful light there – very luminous."

Edward Hopper

The Silent Observer

CAFÉ SCENES

Hopper was not the first artist to paint lonely diners. French Impressionist Edouard Manet tackled the subject 50 years earlier. His subject, like Hopper's, sits with her drink, lost in thought. The sense of isolation is the same but the setting and props are different. For example, the woman below is drinking alcohol rather than a cup of coffee.

▲ Automats were restaurants where pre-packed food and drinks were served by coin-operated machines instead of waiters and waitresses. They first appeared in Philadelphia, Pennsylvania, in 1902, and soon became popular all over the U.S.

▲ *Plum Brandy*, 1877, Edouard Manet. Hopper was interested in the close-up viewpoints of Impressionist paintings such as this one.

Hopper liked to watch people, but more importantly, he liked to watch them without being seen. He spent hours in cafés, restaurants, and diners, making quiet observations. People ate, or drank, or simply sat, without realizing they were being watched. This fascination started early in his life. When Hopper was only 14 years old he sketched two men enjoying a meal together in a restaurant.

LONELY DINER

Hopper painted *Automat*, a familiar New York scene, in 1927. In it he combines two of his favorite subjects – restaurants and solitary figures. Hopper painted isolated, detached people throughout his career – perhaps because, despite his marriage to Jo, that is how he felt. The artist later rejected this view saying, "The loneliness thing is overdone."

TIMELINE ▶

Summer 1928	January 21, 1929	April-May 1929	Summer 1929	October 24, 1929
The Hoppers stay in Gloucester, Massachusetts, then travel to Maine, New Hampshire, and Vermont.	The Frank K. M. Rehn Gallery hosts a solo exhibition of Hopper's work.	The Hoppers visit Charleston, South Carolina.	The Hoppers stay at Two Lights, Cape Elizabeth again.	Wall Street crashes, starting the Great Depression. Millions of people face financial ruin.

Automat, 1927

oil on canvas, 28 $^1/_2$ x 36 in (72.4 x 91.4 cm), Des Moines Art Center, Des Moines, Iowa

Here a woman sits alone at a table. The chair opposite her is unoccupied and the room appears empty. We wonder what she is doing there and who she is waiting to meet. The fact that she still has her hat, coat, and a glove on suggests that she won't be staying long. Hopper captures a private moment in a public place – something we see again and again in his work. The viewer is left to decide what the moment is about.

"If you could say it in words, there'd be no reason to paint."

Edward Hopper

Hopper's New York

New York is a huge city with impressive skyscrapers. It buzzes with activity, noise, and lights. However, this was not Hopper's New York. He was more interested in buildings that could be lived in, streets that could be walked down, and windows that could be looked through.

PORTRAIT OF A STREET

Hopper painted *Early Sunday Morning* at the beginning of the Great Depression – a time of widespread financial hardship. Hopper claimed, the painting was "almost a literal translation of Seventh Avenue."

▲ A street in New York, c.1930. Hopper preferred to paint more approachable scenes such as this one and was unimpressed by the towering skyscrapers being constructed around him.

REALISM

Hopper is considered one of the leading American Realist painters. In its simplest form, Realism means drawing or painting things realistically. In art terms it refers to a 19th-century French movement that rejected idealized styles and subjects in favor of everyday themes shown just as they are. Philadelphia-born Thomas Eakins (1844-1916) trained in Paris during the 1860s. He was heavily influenced by Realist ideas and took them back with him to the United States. Hopper considered Eakins the greatest painter of all, even "greater than Manet." Hopper followed Eakins' lead and became a Realist both in subject matter and style. He painted unglamorous scenes of modern life and treated them in an honest and personal way.

◄ *Between Rounds*, 1880, Thomas Eakins. The intense Realism of many of Eakins' paintings shocked the art world and the public.

TIMELINE ▶

December 1929	1930	1931	1932
Hopper is included in an exhibition called "Paintings by Nineteen Living Americans" at the Museum of Modern Art.	The Hoppers rent Bird Cage Cottage, a house in South Truro, Massachusetts, on a hill overlooking Cape Cod.	Hopper shows work at the First Baltimore Pan-American Exhibition. He spends the summer with Jo at Bird Cage Cottage.	Hopper exhibits in the First Whitney Museum of American Art Biennial.

Early Sunday Morning, 1930

oil on canvas, 35 x 60 in (88.9 x 152.4 cm), Whitney Museum of American Art, New York, New York

Hopper enjoyed using long horizontal formats such as this one. This example suggests that a whole world exists out of view, beyond the edges of the canvas. The buildings are solid, creating a sense of survival and of overcoming hard times. Although the street is empty, in a few hours it will wake up and come alive with the bustle of people and cars. The candy-striped barber's pole, gleaming in the early morning sunshine, will be there to welcome passers-by.

"I spend many days usually before I find a subject that I like well enough to do, and spend a long time on the proportions of the canvas, so that it will do for the design, as nearly as possible what I wish it to do."

Edward Hopper

The New Deal

In 1929 the stock market crashed and the U.S. plunged into the Great Depression. Work was scarce and money was hard to find. People from all walks of life struggled to earn a living. This was especially true for artists whose paintings and sculptures now seemed like unnecessary luxuries.

THE NEW DEAL

On November 8, 1932, Franklin Delano Roosevelt was elected president. He began tackling the country's desperate situation and promised the nation a "New Deal." At this time, thousands of artists were unemployed, unable to feed themselves or their families. In 1933, the government created a program called the Public Works of Art Project to help artists through the difficult economic times. Artists from all over the country were paid a weekly wage to produce works for public buildings.

▲ On October 24th and 29th, 1929, stock prices on Wall Street (the New York Stock Exchange) fell dramatically. Crowds gathered in panic, fearing for their collapsing businesses. Many rich people became penniless overnight. It was the start of the Great Depression.

THE FEDERAL ART PROJECT

Out of the Public Works of Art Project grew the Federal Art Project which ran from 1935 to 1943. It included a number of different programs, each aimed at helping artists through the Depression years. Some artists were employed to make murals and sculptures for buildings such as schools, hospitals, airports, and train stations. Other artists were assigned to the Easel Painting Project and were paid simply to paint. Artists also set up community art centers and galleries in parts of the country where art was virtually unknown.

◄ President Franklin D. Roosevelt brought hope to the people during the Great Depression. In a speech to the nation he declared, "the only thing we have to fear is fear itself."

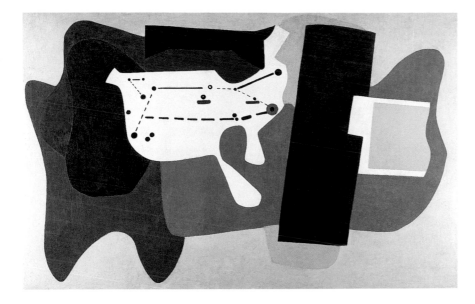

INDEPENDENT SPIRIT

At the time, almost every major artist was involved in the government programs. However, Hopper chose to be different. He was too proud and independent to accept help so he carried on in his own path, painting familiar subjects.

Ironically, the 1930s were boom times for Hopper. The year of the stock market crash, 1929, coincided with his third one-man show. By 1933 he was so famous that the Museum of Modern Art in New York ran a retrospective – an exhibition of his life's works.

Hopper had already suffered his "depression" when nobody bought his art. Now he was flourishing at a time when the rest of the nation was struggling to survive. The following are just a few of the oil paintings he sold in 1929 and 1930:

Light House at Two Lights, $2,000; *Coast Guard Station at Two Lights*, $1,875; *House by an Inlet*, $3,500; *Seventh Avenue Shops* (now called *Early Sunday Morning*), $3,000; *South Truro Church*, $1,800; *Corn Hill, Truro*, $2,000; *Tables for Ladies*, $4,500. He sold even more watercolors.

JACKSON POLLOCK (1912-56)

Abstract Expressionist Jackson Pollock is best known for his dramatic canvases of dripped paint. He worked on the Easel Painting Project for the entire time it was in operation. He was paid an average wage of $95 a month. This secure, paid employment allowed him to explore a range of styles from realistic to abstract before settling on his now famous form of Action Painting.

▲ A photograph of Jackson Pollock in his studio, 1950, by Hans Namuth. Pollock developed a style called Action Painting, in which he splashed or dripped paint onto the canvas.

Cape Cod

Although the 1930s were tough times in the U.S., Hopper's fortunes continued to improve. In 1933 the Hoppers made the biggest investment of their lives. They bought land and built a house in South Truro, on Cape Cod, Massachusetts. From then on, they spent virtually every summer there, enjoying the extraordinary scenery, the brilliant sunlight, and having the space and time to paint.

▲ Hopper outside of his house in South Truro, Massachusetts.

CAPE COD

Cape Cod is a long sliver of land which curves out into the Atlantic Ocean about 249 miles (400 km) along the coast from New York City. It has spectacular scenery with dramatic views across the water.

The Hoppers' large, one bedroom house stands on a piece of land 66 feet (20 m) above sea level. It is surrounded by rolling sandy hills and overlooks Cape Cod Bay. They wanted to create, in Jo's words, "something with the smack of adventure about it."

▶ A boardwalk leading to a lighthouse, Cape Cod. Hopper was fascinated by the light, the scenery, and the man-made structures of Cape Cod.

Cape Cod Evening is one of dozens of paintings reflecting Hopper's summers in Massachusetts. He explained that the scene is not a copy of one place, but pieced together from sketches and impressions of things in the surrounding area.

TIMELINE ▶

November 8, 1932	October 1, 1933	November-December 1933	January 1934	July 1934	1935-39
Franklin D. Roosevelt wins a landslide victory in the presidential elections.	After a brief trip to Canada, the Hoppers buy land in Cape Cod.	Hopper has a retrospective at the Museum of Modern Art, showing 25 oils, 3 watercolors, and 11 etchings.	Hopper has a retrospective at the Arts Club of Chicago.	The Hoppers' studio house at Cape Cod is completed.	The government runs the Federal Art Project to help artists through the Depression years.

Cape Cod Evening, 1939

oil on canvas, 30 ¹/₄ x 40 ¹/₄ in (76.8 x 102.2 cm), National Gallery of Art,
Washington, D.C.

There is an eeriness to this painting, a sense that things are not as they should be.
The couple and their dog are like statues and nature seems to be going wild. The
lawn has become tall and yellow and the surrounding trees seem to be getting
closer and closer. The couple's house is tidy but they are fighting a losing battle.
In this struggle between man and nature, nature is going to win.

"The grove of locust trees was done from sketches
nearby… The figures were done almost entirely without
models, and the dry, blowing grass can be seen from
my studio window in the late summer or autumn."

Edward Hopper

The Movies

HOPPER AND FILMS

Many of Hopper's paintings have been compared to films or stage sets in the way they freeze-frame their subjects and seem to tell a story. The film director Alfred Hitchcock (1899-1980) is said to have got his idea for the house in *Psycho* (1960) from a Hopper painting. He wanted something that looked lonely and created emotion, just as Hopper's scenes do. Like the artist, he chose to peep at intimate worlds through windows. Hitchcock borrowed Hopper's use of light and strong diagonal shadows, and the way he makes people seem dwarfed by landscape and architecture.

▲ By the early 1940s movie theaters such as this one were established in towns across the U.S. They were an increasingly popular source of entertainment at a time when people did not have videos or televisions.

Among the few luxuries which Edward and Jo Hopper enjoyed were the movies and theater. Jo, a former actress, revelled in the make-believe world of cinema and stage. Hopper also enjoyed going to the movies, but for different reasons.

MORE THAN A SHOW

When Hopper visited Paris, his letters home were filled with comments about the plays and films he had seen. For him there was more to the movie theater than just a show. Theater interiors were dark and private places. They allowed him to be an observer – to watch without being seen, to go unnoticed in a crowd as he had done in restaurants. Theaters were also beautiful buildings, another of Hopper's favorite subjects. He painted theater interiors from the late 1920s right until his final work in 1965.

▲ This scene from Hitchcock's *Psycho* (1960) shows hints of Hopper's style.

TIMELINE ▶

1938	April 30, 1939	Summer 1939	September 1, 1939	September 3, 1939
Hopper acquires the rear studio at 3 Washington Square for Jo.	Roosevelt opens the New York World Fair with 60 nations exhibiting their latest technological wonders. Kodak introduces the first color film.	Hopper leaves Cape Cod early to make a trip to Philadelphia.	German Nazi leader Adolf Hitler invades Poland.	Britain and France declare war on Germany at the start of World War II.

New York Movie, 1939

oil on canvas, 32 $^1/_4$ x 40 $^1/_3$ in (81.9 x 101.9 cm), The Museum of Modern Art, New York, New York

Despite its title, this painting is not about a film. Instead, the focus is on the usherette (modeled on a younger version of Jo). Like so many of Hopper's characters, she is in her own world, bored perhaps, or just deep in thought. The lighting in this painting is especially impressive. As Jo noted in her records, there are "Four sources: bracket with three lights, right wall, light inside staircase right, light from lamps underside of boxes, left, and light from screen."

"I've always been interested in light – more than most contemporary painters."

Edward Hopper

On the Road

POP ART

Hopper was one of the first artists to include lettering in his work and consider storefront signs and billboards worth painting. *Gas* is not just a gas station but a tribute to Mobil gas—note both the lettering and the flying horse symbol.

Hopper was starting a trend which was to be taken up by Pop Artists in the late 1950s and '60s. They chose to paint "worthless" objects such as advertisements, comic strips, and billboards – things from popular, or Pop, culture. Andy Warhol (1928-87), with his familiar images of Campbell's soup cans, is probably the most famous of the Pop Artists.

▲ *Soup Can*, 1962, **Andy Warhol.** Warhol made prints of many everyday objects.

Hopper lived in changing times. He watched the development of modern America and two major inventions of his era – cars and movies. Each had a strong influence on his work.

▲ Out on the open road in the late 1940s. The modern car increased people's independence and gave them freedom to travel long distances on newly paved roads.

WHEELS OF FREEDOM

Driving in the United States often involves crossing large stretches of land. Even today it is easy to leave behind the familiar surroundings of the town or city and drive into remote and sparsely populated areas.

The Hoppers bought their first car in 1927, which gave them the opportunity to explore distant places. They escaped the bustle of New York City and traveled to places as far as Canada and California. They even made a number of 2,485-mile (4,000-km) trips to Mexico.

Open spaces dotted with isolated gas stations were a typical sight in Hopper's time and can still be seen today. They inspired his 1940 painting, *Gas* (opposite).

TIMELINE ▶

November 1940	March 1941	Summer 1941	August 1941	December 7, 1941
The Hoppers cut short their vacation to vote against Roosevelt. Nevertheless, Roosevelt is re-elected.	Roosevelt signs the Lend Lease Act, a program which promises aid to the Allies in the war.	The Hoppers drive from Colorado and Utah through the Nevada Desert to California, Oregon, and Wyoming.	Franklin Roosevelt and Winston Churchill sign an alliance between the U.S. and the U.K.	Japan attacks Pearl Harbor.

Gas, 1940

oil on canvas, 26 1/4 x 40 1/4 in (66.7 x 102.2 cm), The Museum of Modern Art, New York, New York

Here, the gas station stands as a bridge between civilization and nature, between the known world and the unknown. The painting, with its illuminated gas pumps, sign, and windows, is set at dusk. Night is slowly replacing the light of day. It is both disturbing – the forest seems alive and frightening – and at the same time comforting, providing an oasis for the lonely traveler at nightfall.

"The thing is that to get to Mexico, all you have to do is put your luggage in your car at the door and drive until you get there – as easy as that!"

Edward Hopper

The Restaurant Theme

The setting for *Nighthawks* may have been inspired by *The Killers* (1927), a short story by the writer Ernest Hemingway (1899-1961). Hemingway wrote in a realistic, detached way which appealed to Hopper. When Hopper read the story for the first time (while working as an illustrator for the magazine in which it was published) he had been so impressed that he'd written to the editors praising its honesty and originality – qualities which are equally true of his own paintings.

By the early 1940s, Edward Hopper's reputation was sealed. The last decade had been a period of successful exhibitions, prizes, and awards from national academies and museums all over the country.

Now he was to revisit a theme that had fascinated him since boyhood – the restaurant interior.

▲ The artist in 1933. By this stage in his life, Hopper was a well-respected figure.

A RECURRING THEME

Nighthawks, with its starkly lit coffee shop and isolated customers, is probably Hopper's most famous work. It combines a number of his favorite themes – solitary people, the loneliness of city life, and the menace of nightfall. Looking at the picture, we feel like we are watching quietly from out in the street, separated from the characters only by the glass of the front window as we pass by. Hopper commented that the scene "was suggested by a restaurant on Greenwich Avenue where two streets meet," but that he had made the restaurant much bigger. This made the figures in *Nighthawks* seem small and vulnerable in relation to their surroundings.

▲ Ernest Hemingway (1899-1961) was an inspirational figure to writers and artists alike. His style, like Hopper's, was calm and to the point.

TIMELINE ▶

1942	1942	Summer 1943	October 1943	August 25, 1944
Hitler sets up death camps for the mass extermination of Jews.	Hopper receives the Ada S. Garrett Prize from the Art Institute of Chicago.	A gas shortage stops the Hoppers from driving to South Truro. They travel by train to Mexico instead.	The Hoppers make a return trip to Saltillo in Mexico.	The Allies liberate Paris, ending the Nazi occupation.

Nighthawks, 1942

oil on canvas, 30 x 56 $^3/_5$ in (76.2 x 144 cm), The Art Institute of Chicago, Chicago, Illinois

In this nighttime scene, a couple sit in the glare of neon light with their mugs of coffee on the bar in front of them. Neither person looks at the other, nor at the man with his back to us. There is also the usual sense of strangeness that we feel in Hopper's paintings. The expression "nighthawks" is similar to "night owls," which means people who operate best after dark. Nighthawks are also actual birds. The male diner has a hooked, hawk-like nose which Jo describes in her notes as a "beak."

"Unconsciously, probably, I was painting the loneliness of a large city."

Edward Hopper

Ignoring the War

In 1941, President Roosevelt and Winston Churchill signed a formal alliance between the United States and the United Kingdom. World War II was being fought in Europe, and the U.S. joined in on the side of the Allies. These huge global events had little impact on Hopper. He chose to ignore politics and world affairs.

CLOSE TO HOME

What mattered to Hopper were his immediate surroundings – in New York, scenes of streets, buildings, and lonely people; in the countryside, stark landscapes with isolated houses and roads. *Rooms for Tourists* was painted the year that Hitler committed suicide, Roosevelt died unexpectedly of a brain hemorrhage, and the war in Europe ended. However, the painting reflects none of these events. It is simply a scene from a car – a snapshot along the road of life.

▲ **Sketch for *Rooms for Tourists*, 1945.** The painting is a portrait of a house in Provincetown, Cape Cod, near where Hopper spent his summers. He went so often to sketch the house that the owners worried about what he was doing.

> *"Great art is the outward expression of an inner life in the artist, and this life will result in his personal vision of the world."*
> *Edward Hopper*

LIFE ON THE MOVE

The invention of the automobile transformed the landscape. It also changed the way people lived. People became dependent on cars. Protected from their surroundings in these bubbles of glass and steel, they became more isolated and detached. In the safety of their cars, motorists watched nature unfold before them like a film on a screen.

Hopper was aware of how lonely life on the road could be. The composition, viewpoint, and framing of his paintings started to resemble what he could see from a car. There is a suggestion in paintings such as *Gas* and *Rooms for Tourists*, that we are merely passing through on our way from one place to another.

TIMELINE ▶

April 1945	May 7, 1945	August 6, 1945	August 15, 1945	1946
Roosevelt dies of a brain hemorrhage. Hitler commits suicide. Hopper wins the Logan Art Institute Medal and Honorarium awarded by The Art Institute of Chicago.	Germany surrenders to the Allies. May 8th is declared VE (Victory in Europe) day. Hopper drives to Saltillo, Mexico, to paint.	The U.S. drops an atomic bomb on Hiroshima, Japan. 80,000 people die.	Japan surrenders to the U.S.	Hopper awarded Honorable Mention at the Art Institute of Chicago.

Rooms for Tourists, 1945
oil on canvas, 30 1/4 x 42 1/3 in (76.8 x 107 cm), Yale University Art Gallery, New Haven, Connecticut

Unlike many of Hopper's buildings, there is nothing sinister about this house – quite the opposite, it is friendly and welcoming. It beckons weary travelers with its brightly lit sign and warm interior lights, offering food, beds, and comfort for the night. The perspective – with the house high up and the gable cut off – suggests that we are looking at it from a car. We are the travelers needing to be rescued.

"To me the most important thing is the sense of going on. You know how beautiful things are when you're traveling."

Edward Hopper

Painting Sunlight

In 1950 the Whitney Museum of American Art in New York held a retrospective of Hopper's work, which moved to Boston and then Detroit in the following months. In the same year, Hopper received an honorary degree from the Art Institute of Chicago. This quiet and shy man was now known throughout the United States.

SIGNS OF SURREALISM

At the age of 80, Hopper was as fascinated with sunlight as he had been in his youthful Paris days. While his interests remained largely the same, his style had developed over the years. *Sun in an Empty Room*, painted in 1963, is about sunlight. It is very different from his handling of *Eleven* A.M. (see page 15), where light streams into a room from a similar angle.

In the work opposite, painted just three years before he died, the room is stripped to the bare essentials. It is one of the most "surreal" of Hopper's paintings, and could almost be a scene from a dream.

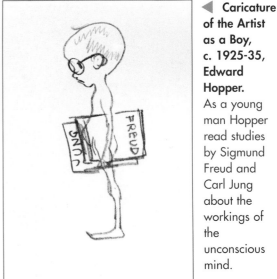

◀ **Caricature of the Artist as a Boy, c. 1925-35, Edward Hopper.**
As a young man Hopper read studies by Sigmund Freud and Carl Jung about the workings of the unconscious mind.

Although Hopper is considered a Realist, the meanings of his paintings go deeper than the surface of the canvas. Hopper wanted to convey his state of mind. As he put it, "I'm after ME."

SURREALISM

Surrealism was a movement in art and literature which flourished in Europe in the 1920s and '30s. Surrealists were interested in unconscious thoughts more than conscious realities. Their paintings tended to be bizarre and illogical like dreams. They also seemed to have hidden meanings, but it was up to the viewer to decide what those were. Among the leading Surrealist artists were Salvador Dali (1904-89) and René Magritte (1898-1967).

◀ *L'Empire des Lumieres II*, **René Magritte, 1950.**
This picture is hard to understand. Is it day or night?

TIMELINE ▶

February 1950	April 1950	June 1950	1952	1952	1953	1955
The Whitney Museum holds a retrospective of Hopper's work.	Retrospective moves to the Boston Museum of Fine Arts.	Retrospective moves to the Detroit Institute of Arts.	Hopper makes a third trip to Mexico, including a visit to Santa Fe.	Hopper is one of the four artists chosen to represent the U.S at the prestigious Venice Biennale.	Hemingway wins the Nobel Prize for Literature for his novel *A Farewell to Arms*.	Hopper is made a member of the American Academy of Arts and Letters.

Sun in an Empty Room, 1963
oil on canvas, 28 ³/₄ x 39 ³/₈ in (73 x 100 cm), Private collection

Hopper has left out all unnecessary details in this painting – there's nothing to distract our eye. In a preliminary sketch he had planned to include a figure but there is no trace of human presence here. The building stands alone, undisturbed except by the gentle rustle of trees outside. It is a painting about light and nature in its most peaceful form.

"Maybe I am not very human. What I wanted to do was paint sunlight on the side of a house."

Edward Hopper

The Final Curtain

◀ Hopper working at an easel in his studio, 1963. Jo looks on.

CLOWNS

A clown is featured in one of Hopper's earliest works, *Soir Bleu* (page 11), and in his last, *Two Comedians*. In both cases the clown represents the artist. In *Soir Bleu*, he is weary. He sits in a café surrounded by a cast of characters – the rich, the poor, the elegant, and the lost. He reminds us of a clown painted 200 years earlier by Antoine Watteau (1684-1721), which Hopper would have seen at the Louvre in Paris. In contrast, Hopper's final work is not sad at all. The clowns here have done what they set out to do. They have entertained, and this is their goodbye, their final curtain.

Hopper's later years brought more achievements – prizes, awards, and major retrospectives – too numerous to list. He continued as he always had, living his simple life with Jo at Washington Square in New York, spending summers in New England, and painting. Unlike most artists, Hopper's work changed very little during his lifetime and there was nothing new about his choice of subject in the years before he died.

FOND FAREWELL

In 1964, illness briefly stopped Hopper from working. The following year, at age 83, he painted *Two Comedians*, his farewell to the world. In it he presents himself and Jo, dressed as two pantomime clowns, bowing gracefully to their audience at the end of their performance. Hopper died less than two years after completing this painting and his devoted wife Jo died the following year.

▲ *Gilles*, 1718-20, Antoine Watteau. As he faces the audience, Watteau's clown gives the feeling of being isolated, the odd one out.

TIMELINE ▶

October-November 1962	July-November 1963	1964	1965	May 15, 1967
The Philadelphia Museum of Art shows Hopper's Complete Graphic Work.	Arizona Art Gallery, South Truro, stages a Hopper retrospective.	Hopper becomes too ill to paint. The Whitney Museum organizes a large retrospective exhibition which then moves to Chicago, Detroit, and St Louis.	Hopper completes his final painting, *Two Comedians*.	Edward Hopper dies in his home at 3 Washington Square North.

Two Comedians, 1965

oil on canvas, 29 x 40 in (73.7 x 101.6 cm), Collection Mr. & Mrs. Frank Sinatra

Jo found this painting very moving. While the performers are clearly on a stage the green on the right suggests trees and the dark blue behind them is like the black of the night. They stand frozen in the spotlights, about to retreat into darkness. We get the feeling that this is their final "encore" – they won't come back again.

"In every artist's development the germ of the later work is always found in the earlier. What he once was, he always is."

Edward Hopper

Hopper's Legacy

Despite the extraordinary popularity of Hopper's work, few painters have followed in his footsteps. Perhaps he was just too much of an individual, producing work that others couldn't match.

One exception is Robert Cottingham (b.1935) who credits Hopper as a major inspiration. He is famous for a style called Photorealism – painting in such a detailed way that the works look like photographs.

Cottingham claims to have seen every one of Hopper's works in New York City. He also likes to paint everyday subjects including neon shop signs, lights, and logos, which he views as "emblems of America."

▲ *Barber Shop*, **1998, Robert Cottingham.** The influence of *Early Sunday Morning* (page 23), Cottingham's favorite Hopper piece, is clear in this painting of a striped barbershop pole.

▼ *The Restaurant Window I*, **1967, George Segal.** Artist Mark Rothko (1903-70) called Segal's works "paintings you could walk into." Segal didn't like this idea but the similarity between his work and that of Hopper is unmistakable.

NEW DIMENSIONS

Hopper's legacy stretches far beyond the painted canvas. American sculptor George Segal (b.1924) is an artist who seems to have turned Hopper's ideas into three-dimensional form. Segal makes life-size plaster casts of people, and places them in typical Hopper settings such as doorways, gas stations, theaters, and restaurants. Like Hopper, he captures the loneliness of big-city life.

FREEZE-FRAMED

Hopper has also influenced photography and, to an even greater extent, filmmakers. Famous names such as Alfred Hitchcock, Dennis Potter (1935-94), and Wim Wenders (b.1945) were all great admirers of Hopper's work and chose to base scenes in their films around some of his paintings. *Nighthawks*, for example (see page 33), can be seen in both Dennis Potter's film *Pennies from Heaven* (1978) and Wim Wenders' *The End of Violence* (1997).

When we remember how much Edward Hopper was influenced by the movies, it is interesting to see how the source of inspiration from films to paintings and back to films again has come full circle.

> *"An Edward Hopper painting is like the opening paragraph of a story. A car will drive up to a filling station, and the driver will have a bullet in his belly… like the beginnings of American films."*
>
> *Wim Wenders*

WHITNEY MUSEUM

The best place to see works by Hopper is the Whitney Museum in New York City. Jo Hopper bequeathed all her husband's work to the Whitney after he died.

▶ A scene from Dennis Potter's film *Pennies from Heaven*, 1978. The setup is almost identical to Hopper's painting *Nighthawks* (page 33).

Artistic Accounts

Jo N. Hopper, as she referred to herself, started keeping detailed notes, or "ledgers," of all her husband's work after they married in 1924. She bought cheap account books and set out to write notes "at the time each work is finished, or before it leaves the studio."

"Gas, Oct. 9, 40 brought back to N.Y. on hasty trip home to register for Willkie Late twilight. Hanging sign 'Mobil oil' white with red horse lit from above, red pumps (3) with lamps lit, throwing light on putty colored pavement ground... Blond man in blue pants, white shirt, black vest tending pump..."

▲ **This is typical of Jo's notes in the ledgers. She describes the scene in detail, as if she is analyzing the painting.**

Her goal was to include in her notes the title, the date of completion, a brief description of the work, the sale price, and the buyer. Fortunately for us she ended up including a great deal more, cataloging Hopper's paintings going back as far as 1907.

DETAILED NOTES

Hopper illustrated all of his paintings and etchings in the ledgers, paying more attention to detail as time went on. He noted the materials he used and any other points that interested him. Jo included lists of newspaper and magazine articles about his work, as well as making occasional diary-type entries.

◄ **Artist's Ledger – Book III, 1924-67. p.31, *High Noon*.**
Hopper notes here how he made a model of the house in this painting so that he could see exactly how the light and shadows fell on the walls.

TIMELINE ▶

1882	1909	1917	1923	1926
1882 Edward Hopper is born in Nyack, New York.	**1909** Visits Paris. Paints outdoors by River Seine.	**1917** Exhibits at First Annual Exhibition of the American Society of Independent Artists. U.S. declares war on Germany.	**1923** Shows at Exhibition of Etchers, Art Institute of Chicago. Wins Logan prize. Makes second sale, *The Mansard Roof*, to Brooklyn Museum.	**1926** "Exhibition of Water-colors and Etchings by Edward Hopper," St. Botolph Club, Boston.
1899–1900 Attends New York's Correspondence School of Illustrating.	**1910** Shows at an "Exhibition of Independent Artists" in New York.	**1918** Exhibits etchings. Wins first prize for war poster *Smash the Hun*.	**1924** Marries Jo Nivison. Sells 16 watercolors and gives up commercial work.	**1927** Hoppers buy a car.
1900-06 Attends the New York School of Art.	**1913** Sells his first work, *Sailing*. Moves to 3 Washington Square North.	**1918** End of World War I.	**1925** Shows at 10th Annual Exhibition of the Whitney Studio Club.	**1928** Hopper makes final print.
1906 Works in New York as a commercial artist. Travels to Paris.	**1914** World War I breaks out in Europe.	**1920** Hopper's first one-man show at the Whitney Studio Club, New York.		**1929** Frank K.M. Rehn Gallery hosts one-artist show of Hopper's work. Wall Street crashes.
1907 Returns to New York.	**1915** Hopper takes up etching. Exhibits *Soir Bleu*.			

▼ Jo talks about the setting for *Nighthawks* (page 33). She is clearly interested in the bright colors of the restaurant interior in contrast to the darkness of the night.

> *"Night Hawks Finished Jan 21, 1942 Night & brilliant interior of cheap restaurant. Bright items: cherry wood counters & tops of surrounding stools; lights on metal tanks at rear right; brilliant streak of jade green tiles 3/4 across canvas at base of glass of curving window at corner…"*

> *"Rooms for Tourists Finished in S. Truro studio, Sept, 1945. To Rehn Gallery Nov. 8 1945 White house (grey) in black night, seen by electric street lamps (offstage R.) Sign 'Rooms,' lower shafts of door stoop, bit of railing extreme lower L. Light white…"*

▲ Here Jo gives us a glimpse of what is not seen in the painting – the source of light, which is a set of street lamps to the right of the scene, beyond the edge of the canvas.

DIFFERING STYLES

Keeping the journals was a joint effort. While Hopper made the drawings, Jo did most of the writing; together they constructed the "stories." The way they approached the ledgers reveals their very different personalities. Hopper's entries are graphic, relying on his sketches to speak for themselves. Jo writes down all sorts of little details, as chatty and informal in her note-keeping as in her life.

By the time they finished there were three full account books and two partially filled ones, one of which was entirely devoted to Hopper's etchings.

> *"Jo Painting, Feb 25, '36 Head against light; warm flesh tones against white background (painted on white canvas). Grey wool blue dress with whitish crash collar, silver brooch with green stone center. Hair darkish brown & very bushy, just having been washed & waiting to dry thoroughly."* JH

> *"Given to wife, Jo N Hopper as anniversary present   1955"* EH

▲ Jo describes a portrait Hopper painted of her in 1936. She gives a descriptive account, noting the state of her hair and clothes. Hopper adds just a simple line below.

1932	1934	1942	1945	1952
1932 Hopper takes extra studio space at 3 Washington Square North. Exhibits at First Whitney Museum of American Art Biennial. Franklin D. Roosevelt wins presidential elections in landslide victory.	**1934** Retrospective at the Arts Club of Chicago. Cape Cod house finished.	**1942** Hopper receives the Ada S. Garrett Prize from the Art Institute of Chicago.	**1945** Germany and then Japan surrender to the Allies. End of World War II.	**1952** Hopper exhibits at the Venice Biennale.
	1935-39 U.S. government runs Federal Art Project.	**1943** Gas shortage stops Hoppers from driving to South Truro. They go by train to Mexico instead.	**1946** Hopper awarded Honorable Mention at Art Institute of Chicago. Travels again to Mexico.	**1955** Elected a member of the American Academy of Arts and Letters.
1933 Hoppers buy land in South Truro, Cape Cod, to build a house. Retrospective exhibition at Museum of Modern Art.	**1938** Hopper acquires rear studio at 3 Washington Square for Jo.	**1945** Hopper awarded the Logan Art Institute Medal and Honorarium. Elected member of the National Institute of Arts and Letters. Drives to Saltillo, Mexico.	**1950** Whitney Museum stages a retrospective of Hopper's work	**1962** Andy Warhol paints Campbell's Soup Cans. Philadelphia Museum of Art shows Hopper's Complete Graphic Work.
	1939 World War II starts in Europe.		**1952** Hopper makes third trip to Mexico and visits Santa Fe, New Mexico.	**1967** Edward Hopper dies at his studio at 3 Washington Square North.
	1941 Hoppers go on driving trip around U.S.			

Glossary

Abstraction: an art movement which was influential between 1910 and 1920. Abstract art does not imitate the world around us – it is often impossible to recognize objects, people, or places. Wassily Kandinsky (1866-1944) and Piet Mondrian (1872-1944) were both leading Abstract artists.

Ashcan School: a school of painting which focused on ordinary, everyday subjects. It was founded by Robert Henri (1865-1929) and included William Glackens (1870-1938), George Luks (1867-1933), and John Sloan (1871-1951).

automat: a popular place to eat in the 1940s and '50s, where the food is sold by coin-operated vending machines.

Baptist: a form of the Protestant faith, or someone who practices it.

Biennale: an important international art exhibition held in Venice every two years. The first one was in 1895.

Bohemian: describes a person, often an artist or intellectual, who lives in a way that does not follow social conventions.

canvas: a woven cloth used as a surface for paintings.

Cubism: the name of an art movement based in Paris from about 1907, led by Georges Braque (1882-1963) and Pablo Picasso (1881-1973). The Cubists painted multiple viewpoints of a person or object so they were all seen at once.

death camp: a prison camp where prisoners are sent for execution.

easel: a stand for a canvas to rest on so the artist can paint easily.

etching: a print on paper made from an etched metal plate.

Fauvism: a style of painting, based on intense, unnatural colors, which flourished in Paris from about 1905 to 1907. Henri Matisse (1869-1954) is considered the original "Fauve."

Federal Art Project: a program run by the government from 1935 to 1943 to help artists through the difficult times of the Great Depression.

freeze-framing: a technique of stopping a film so that you see a single camera shot, or a frozen moment in time.

graphic design: drawing, lettering, and illustration.

Great Depression: the name given to the global economic slump of the 1930s.

immigrants: people who have left their homeland and arrived in a new country to live. Thousands of immigrants flocked to the U.S. between 1870 and 1916.

Impressionism: a style of painting that originated in Paris in the late 19th century. Impressionists painted "impressions" of the world with broad brushstrokes of pure color. The group included Claude Monet (1840-1926), Auguste Renoir (1841-1919), and Edgar Degas (1834-1917).

mural: a painting done on a wall.

nighthawk: the name of a type of bird and a term used for a person who works at night.

Photorealism: (also called Superrealism), a style of painting that represented objects in minute detail, sometimes based on photographic images.

Pop Art: the art movement that flourished in the United States in the 1960s which sought to make art more popular by featuring everyday objects, famous people, or well-known designs. Andy Warhol (1928-87) was one of the most famous Pop artists.

Public Works of Art Project: one of the government-funded programs to help artists through the Depression years. Artists were involved in producing murals and sculptures for public buildings, or simply painting for a wage in the Easel Painting Project.

Realism: a style of painting in which artists attempt to portray things accurately, or "realistically." Thomas Eakins (1844-1916) was the leader of American Realism.

retrospective: an exhibition looking back at an artist's life work.

surreal: strange and dreamlike.

Surrealism: an art movement that emerged in the 1920s and tried to depict the life of our unconscious minds, or dreams. Its most famous artist was Salvador Dali (1904-89).

Symbolism: an art movement that flourished toward the end of the 19th century that tried to give feelings, such as love and hate, a visual form in a drawing or on a canvas. The individual style of the Symbolist painters varied greatly.

Museums and Galleries

You can see Hopper's work throughout the United States. The Whitney Museum of American Art has the largest collection, with more than 2,500 oil paintings, watercolors, drawings, and prints – but there are others, some of which are listed below. If you can't get to any of these galleries yourself, you may be able to visit their web sites. Gallery web sites often show pictures of the artworks they have on display. Some of the web sites even offer virtual tours which allow you to wander around and look at different paintings while sitting comfortably in front of your computer!

Art Institute of Chicago
111 South Michigan Avenue
Chicago, IL 60603-6110
www.artic.edu

Butler Institute of American Art
524 Wick Avenue
Youngstown, OH 44502
www.butlerart.com

Carnegie Museum of Art
4400 Forbes Avenue
Pittsburgh, PA 15213-4080
www.cmoa.org

Cleveland Museum of Art
11150 East Boulevard
Cleveland, OH 44106
www.clevelandart.org

Dayton Art Institute
456 Belmonte Park North
Dayton, OH 45405-4700
www.daytonartinstitute.org

Delaware Art Museum
2301 Kentmere Parkway
Wilmington, DE 19806
www.delart.mus.de.us

Hirshhorn Museum and Sculpture Garden
Independence Avenue at Seventh Street SW
Washington, D.C. 20013-7012
www.hirshhorn.si.edu

Indianapolis Museum of Art
1200 West 38th Street
Indianapolis, IN 46208-4196
www.ima-art.org

Metropolitan Museum of Art
1000 Fifth Avenue at 82nd Street
New York, NY 10028-0198
www.metmuseum.org

Montclair Art Museum
3 South Mountain Avenue
Montclair, NJ 07042-1747
www.montclair-art.com

Museum of Fine Arts, Boston
465 Huntington Avenue
Boston, MA 02115-5523
www.mfa.org

Museum of Modern Art
(Under renovation until 2005.
See web site for further details.)
11 West 53rd Street
New York, NY 10019
www.moma.org

National Gallery of Art
Sixth and Constitution Avenue NW
Washington, D.C. 20565
www.nga.gov

San Diego Museum of Art
1450 El Prado
San Diego, CA 92101
www.sdmart.org

Whitney Museum of American Art
945 Madison Avenue at 75th Street
New York, NY 10021
www.whitney.org

Index

Abstraction 9, 44
Action painting 25
Ashcan School 7, 44
Automat 20, 21
automats 20, 44
Aviation: Evolution of Forms Under Aerodynamic Limitations (Gorky) 25

Barber Shop (Cottingham) 40
Betwen Rounds (Eakins) 22
buildings 14, 18, 19, 23, 24, 25, 28, 34, 35, 37

cafés 9, 11, 20, 28, 32, 40
Cape Cod 26-27
Cape Cod Evening 26, 27
Cape Elizabeth 18
Caricature of the Artist as a Boy 36
cars 17, 30, 34, 35
Cézanne, Paul 9
city 15, 22, 32, 33, 34, 40
clowns 11, 16, 38, 39
Cottingham, Robert 40
Courbet, Gustave 9
Cubism 9, 44

Dali, Salvador 36, 44
Degas, Edgar 9, 44

Eakins, Thomas 22
Early Sunday Morning 22, 23, 25, 40
Easel Painting Project 24, 25, 44
Edward Hopper at His Easel, (Nivison) 17
Eleven A.M. 14, 15, 36
L'Empire des Lumières II (Magritte) 36
etchings 12-13, 14, 16, 42, 44

Fauvism 9, 44
Federal Art Project 24, 25, 44
film 16, 28, 29, 30, 34, 41

Gas 30, 31, 34, 42
Gilles (Watteau) 38
Gorky, Arshile 25
Great Depression 22, 24-25, 26, 44

Hemingway, Ernest 32
Henri, Robert 7, 16, 44
High Cliff, Coast of Maine (Homer) 18
High Noon 42
Hitchcock, Alfred 28, 41
Homer, Winslow 18
Hopper, Edward
    appearance of 7
    education 6, 7, 8
    home 6, 10, 18, 22, 26
    as an illustrator 8, 10, 12, 13, 14, 32
    influence of 28, 30, 40-41
    influences on 9, 11, 20, 22, 32, 41
    light, use of 9, 12, 14, 18, 19, 22, 28, 29, 33, 35, 36, 37, 39
    and loneliness 15, 20, 28, 31, 32, 33, 34, 40
    marriage 14, 17, 20, 42
    and movies (see *film*)
    and politics 13, 25, 34
    style of art 6, 7, 9, 10, 12, 14, 18, 20, 22, 28, 32, 34, 36, 38, 40, 41
    and travel 8, 9, 30, 31, 35
Hopper, Jo (wife) 14, 16-17, 20, 26, 28, 38, 42, 43

Impressionism 9, 10, 19, 44

ledgers 16, 42-43
Light at Two Lights 19

MacDowell Club, New York 11
Magritte, René 36
Manet, Edouard 9, 19, 22
The Mansard Roof 18
Matisse, Henri 9, 44
Monet, Claude 9, 44
Moreau, Gustave 10

New Deal, The 24
New York Movie 29
New York School of Art 7, 8, 16
Nighthawks 32, 33, 41, 43
Nivison, Jo (see *Hopper, Jo*)

Paris 8-9, 28, 36
Pegasus Triumphant (Redon) 10
Pène du Bois, Guy 7
Pennies from Heaven (film) 41
photography 40, 41
Photorealism 40
Picasso, Pablo 9, 44
Pissarro, Camille 9, 44
Plum Brandy (Manet) 20
Pollock, Jackson 25
Pop art 30, 44
prizes 13, 32, 38
Public Works of Art Project 24, 44

Realism 6, 9, 22, 36, 44
Redon, Odilon 10
restaurants (see *cafés*)
The Restaurant Window I (Segal) 40
retrospectives 25, 36, 38, 44
Rooms for Tourists 34, 35, 43
Roosevelt, Franklin D. 24

Segal, George 40
Sloan, John 7, 44
Smash the Hun 13
Soir Bleu 10, 11, 38
Sun in an Empty Room 36, 37
Surrealism 36, 44
Symbolism 10, 44

theater 16, 28
Two Comedians 38, 39

Wall Street Crash 24-25
Warhol, Andy 30, 44
watercolors 9, 14, 17, 18, 25
Waterloo Bridge, Cloudy Day (Monet) 9
Watteau, Antoine 38
Whitney Studio Club 13
A Woman's Work (Sloan) 7
World War I 12, 13
World War II 34